Handling Data

David Kirkby

RIGBY
INTERACTIVE
LIBRARY

Designed by The Point
Cover design by Pinpoint Design
Printed in the United States of America

00 99 98 97 96
10 9 8 7 6 5 4 3 2 1

Library of Congress Cataloging-in-Publication Data
Kirkby, David, 1943–
    Handling data / David Kirkby.
      p. cm. — (Math live)
    Includes index.
    Summary: Introduces elementary statistical concepts along with simple activities and calculations.
    ISBN 1-57572-046-9
    1. Statistics—Juvenile literature.   2. Statistics—Graphic methods—Juvenile literature.   [1. Statistics.]   I. Title.
    II. Series: Kirkby, David, 1943–   Math live.
    QA276.13.K57   1996
    519.5—dc20   95–33559
                                        CIP
                                        AC

Acknowledgments
The author and publisher wish to acknowledge, with thanks, the following photographic sources:
Ace Photo Agency, p. 12; Zefa, p. 20; Anthony Blake, p. 6; Trevor Clifford, pp. 19, 24, 40; Chris Honeywell, p. 38.

The publisher would also like to thank the following for the kind loan of equipment:
NES Arnold Ltd; Polydron International Ltd.

Note to the Reader
In this book some words are printed in **bold** type. This indicates that the word is listed in the glossary on page 44. The glossary gives a brief explanation of words that may be new to you.

CONTENTS

1 DATA

We often have to deal with information and try to sort it out. When we have some facts that give us information about something, we call it **data**.

One way of collecting data is by observation. For example, in a traffic survey, we might watch the traffic and observe the different types of vehicle using a road.

Traffic Survey	
Cars	I I I I
Trucks	I
Bicycles	I
Motorcycles	
Buses	I I
Others	

As we observe, we will need to record the data, so that it can be remembered and used later. The recording of data is done on a **data collection sheet**.

Another way of collecting data is by measuring. For example, if we are studying trees, we might need to collect data by measuring the lengths of their leaves.

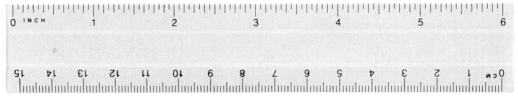

Sometimes data is collected by asking people questions. The questions need to be carefully planned beforehand. The set of questions is called a **questionnaire**.

When the data has been collected and recorded, it is often confused and needs to be made simpler. This is called processing the data. Much **data processing** is done by a computer.

CAR database.<100%>

	Time	1:31:52 p.m.	1:36:14 p.m.	1:41:35 p.m.	1:48:22 p.m.	1:55:10 p.m.
	Type of car	Sedan	Hatchback	Van	Sedan	Sedan
	Color	Red	Black	Silver	Red	Blue
	Year	1988	1994	1991	1992	1992

When the data has been processed, we look for ways of representing it. **Data representation** means showing it to other people in an easy-to-read way.

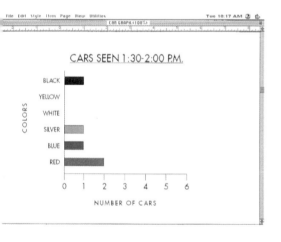

CAR GRAPH.<100%>

CARS SEEN 1:30-2:00 P.M.

Usually this is by means of graphs, pictures, and charts. When we look at the represented data, whether it is our own data or someone else's, we need to be able to "read" it and understand what it tells us. This is called **interpreting** the data.

In summary, there are five stages of handling data. They are collecting data, recording data, processing data, representing data, and interpreting data.

Data is all around us—on television, in newspapers, in magazines, in stores—and it is a part of everybody's life, both at work and at home. It is therefore important to be skilled in handling it.

PICTOGRAPHS

A **pictograph** is a graph that uses pictures to show information.

A store had a special offer last Wednesday. They offered a free ice cream cone to each of the first twenty shoppers. They could choose from four flavors: strawberry, vanilla, mint, and chocolate. The pictograph below shows the chosen flavors.

<u>Choice of Flavor of Ice Cream</u>

Strawberry	🍦 🍦 🍦 🍦
Vanilla	🍦 🍦 🍦 🍦 🍦 🍦 🍦 🍦
Mint	🍦 🍦 🍦 🍦 🍦
Chocolate	🍦 🍦 🍦

Key: 🍦 means 1 ice cream

There are four pictures next to the strawberry flavor to show that four shoppers chose that flavor. The **key** shows what each picture means. All pictographs must have a key.

TO DO

- How many shoppers chose mint flavor?
- Which flavor was most popular?

Some children were asked to choose their favorite season. This pictograph shows the results.

Our Favorite Season

Spring ⚇⚇⚇⚇

Summer ⚇⚇⚇⚇⚇

Autumn ⚇⚇⚇

Winter ⚇⚇   Key: ⚇ means 2 votes

It is common to draw a pictograph in which a picture means more than 1. The key explains that one picture means 2 votes, so that half a picture means 1 vote. The three and a half pictures next to "spring" show that seven children voted for this season.

How many voted for each of the other seasons?
How many children voted altogether?

TO DO

Play the Pictograph Game.

You need a deck of cards, shuffled and placed in a pile facedown

- Choose two suits each (from hearts, clubs, diamonds, spades).
- Turn over the top card and draw the shape of a card in the correct line.
- Continue revealing cards and drawing pictures.
- The winner is the person who chose the first suit to have five pictures.
- Play a variation in which you draw half a card each time.

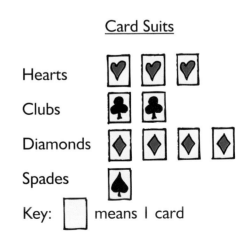

Card Suits

Hearts

Clubs

Diamonds

Spades

Key: means I card

7

3 TALLIES

When some data has been collected, it may need processing. This data shows how many slices of bread were eaten by each of 60 children in one day.

Number of Slices of Bread Eaten Yesterday

0	1	3	2	6	4	5	0	4	2
4	2	3	5	4	5	3	4	5	3
5	3	4	5	4	2	6	3	4	4
3	6	5	3	6	0	5	4	6	2
5	4	2	6	4	6	1	4	3	5
6	3	5	0	4	4	5	3	2	4

One way of processing data is to draw a **tally chart**. We make a line for each number and complete a "gate" to show a group of five lines. These lines are called **tallies**.

Number of Slices Eaten	Tallies	Total
0	I I I I	4
1	I I	2
2	++++ I I	7
3	++++ ++++ I	11
4	++++ ++++ ++++ I	16
5	++++ ++++ I I	12
6	++++ I I I	8

By counting the tallies, we can easily count the total number of children who ate no slices of bread, one slice of bread, two slices of bread, and so on.

TO DO

- How many children ate three slices of bread yesterday?
- What was the most common number of slices eaten?
- How many children ate less than three slices?

8

A group of children found out the ages of all the people in their families. Altogether there were 83 people. Here are their ages.

Ages of People in Our Families

11	30	7	42	28	20	52	45	39	54	8	41	38	25	15
24	32	50	1	59	23	82	36	12	69	21	73	5	49	38
14	42	29	12	30	1	21	75	27	60	4	48	37	53	36
31	6	67	39	21	55	34	2	74	35	58	17	61	23	30
22	53	24	44	3	9	40	26	64	34	65	48	7	31	25
			46	77	20	33	57	13	46	32				

Because there are so many different ages, it is best to group the data into different age-ranges.

Age-range	Tallies	Frequency
0–9	++++ ++++ I	11
10–19	++++ II	7
20–29	++++ ++++ ++++ I	16
30–39	++++ ++++ ++++ III	18
40–49	++++ ++++ I	11
50–59	++++ IIII	9
60–69	++++ I	6
70–79	IIII	4
80–89	I	1

Notice that each group of ages is the same size—ten years. The word "total" is sometimes replaced by the word "frequency." **Frequency** means "how many" or "how often." When the data is put into groups like this, it is called **grouped data**.

CHALLENGE

How good are you at reading the grouped data tally chart?
- To which age-range do the most people belong?
- How many age-ranges contain more than ten people?
- How many people are aged 40 or more?
- How many people are aged less than 20?

BLOCK GRAPHS

A **graph** is a picture that makes data clearer and easier to read and understand. A **block graph** is the simplest type of graph. It is made with a collection of blocks. Each block stands for something.

A block graph can be shown using objects such as cubes. The data below shows the hair color of a group of children. One cube represents one child with that color of hair.

A simple way of drawing a block graph is to use gummed squares.

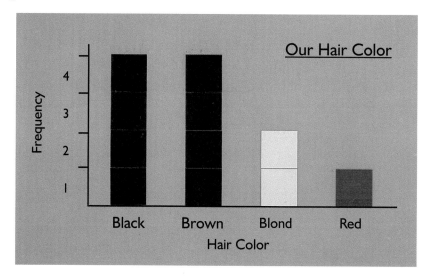

Each square represents one child. Each square is a "block" on the block graph.

The graph on page 10 has a horizontal and a vertical line that are labeled "Hair Color" and "Frequency." Each line is called an **axis** of the graph. Together they are called **axes**.

The **horizontal axis** shows the hair color. The **vertical axis** shows the frequency, or the number of children with each hair color.

In a block graph, the numbering of the frequencies on the vertical axis should be written in the spaces between the blocks.

Notice that the graph has a title. All block graphs should have a title, and both axes should be clearly labeled. There should also be spaces of equal width between each column of blocks.

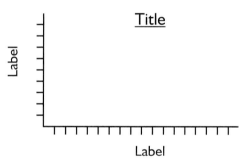

It is important to be able to "read" or interpret a graph, to understand what the graph shows.

TO DO

Use the graph on page 10 to answer these questions:
- How many of the children have blond hair?
- Which hair color is the most frequent?
- How many more children have black than red hair?
- How many children altogether are in the group?

CHALLENGE

Look at this block graph.

Can you invent five questions for this graph? Try them out on a friend.

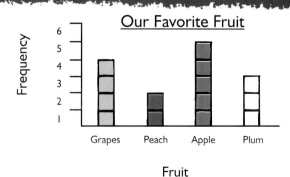

5 BAR GRAPHS

A **bar graph** shows information using bars. It is similar to a block graph, but uses a bar to replace each tower of blocks. Block graphs and bar graphs are often used to show differences between things.

John watched cars traveling past his house and wrote down the color of each. He watched 40 cars altogether and recorded his data in a tally chart.

Color of Cars Passing my House		
Car Color	Tallies	Frequency
Red	⊬⊬ ⊬⊬ |||	13
White	⊬⊬ |||	8
Black	⊬⊬ ⊬⊬	10
Blue	⊬⊬	5
Green	||||	4

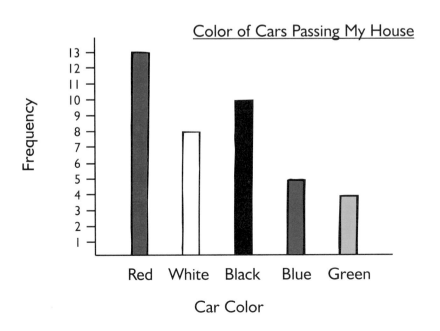

Color of Cars Passing My House

As with a block graph, a bar graph must have a title and two labeled axes. The length of the bars shows how many or how much.

The bars should all be the same width and have gaps of equal width between them.

TO DO

- Collect your own data on car color and draw a bar graph to show the results.
- Compare it with the graph on page 12.
- Was red the most popular color in your survey?

A bar graph is sometimes known as a **bar chart**. For a block graph, the numbering of the frequencies was written between the spaces. For a bar graph, the numbering should be written next to the axis divisions.

CHALLENGE

23 children were asked their favorite kind of cookie.

- Chocolate chip was the most popular, with seven votes.
- Oatmeal was the least popular, with only one vote.
- Twice as many voted for date bars as voted for shortbread.
- Twice as many voted for wafers as voted for ginger cookies.

Can you draw the bar graph to show the results?

BAR GRAPHS WITH LINES

A **bar graph with lines** is similar to a bar graph except that instead of drawing a bar to show the frequency, we draw a straight line.

In written texts, some letters are used more often than others. The graph below shows the frequency of each letter used in the passage of writing below left.

Take a closer look at the buttons on your shirt. Girls' clothes usually button up from the left. But boys' clothes button up from the other side. Can you guess why?

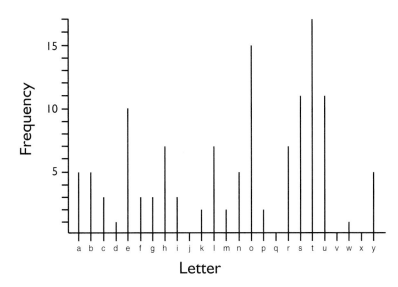

Use of Letters in the Passage

The lengths of the bars match the frequency with which each letter occurs.

CHALLENGE

- Choose a book.
- Look at the first 200 words (of two letters or more) in the book.
- Investigate how often each letter of the alphabet is used.
- Look at the scores for each letter in this word game.
- What scores are given to the most frequently used letters? Why do you think this is?

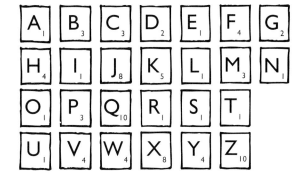

Bar graphs and bar graphs with lines are usually drawn so that the bars are **vertical**, but sometimes they are **horizontal**.

Dates of a Bag of Coins

Coin Date

1990
1991
1992
1993
1994
1995

Frequency
2   4   6   8   10   12

The graph shows that the most common date on the coins is 1993, and the least common is 1990. No coins were found to be more than six years old.

TO DO

- Collect as many coins as you can and draw a bar graph with lines to show the dates of the coins.
- Use graph paper to draw the graph. Start by drawing the axes in the same position as those in the picture above. Sort your coins into piles for each year, count the number in each pile, then draw the lines on the graph.
- Write about your discoveries.
- Compare the dates of coins of different values.

7 LINE GRAPHS

A **line graph** is often used to show changes or trends over a period of time, for example, with temperature.
In these cases the horizontal axis is "time."

Imagine that the data is represented by a bar graph with lines, then the tops of the lines in the graph are joined by a series of straight lines, and the bar lines removed. The result is a line graph.

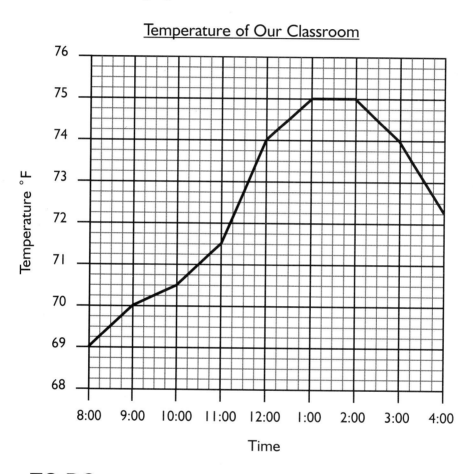

TO DO

Use the graph to answer these questions.
• What was the temperature at 9:00 and at 2:00?
• At what times was the temperature 74°F?
• What was the change in temperature between 10:00 and 11:00?
• At what time was the classroom the hottest?

16

We can draw a line graph to show a journey.

The vertical axis shows the distance from the start in miles. The horizontal axis shows the time of the day. These graphs are often called **distance-time graphs**.

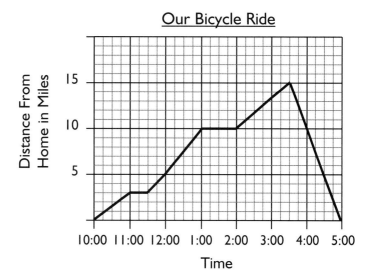

Our Bicycle Ride

The graph shows that the bicycle ride started at 10:00 and that 3 miles were traveled in the first hour. Between 11:00 and 11:30, the horizontal line shows that no miles were cycled and that the cyclists stopped for a rest. The journey then continued for 2 miles in the next half an hour.

TO DO

Describe the rest of the journey.

CHALLENGE

Invent a story to match this graph.

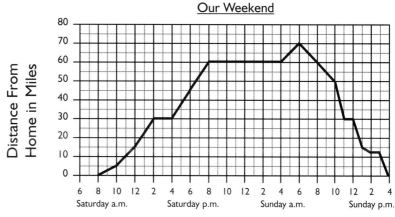

Our Weekend

PIE CHARTS

A **pie chart** is another example of a picture that compares data. It shows how the total amount of something is divided. It is a circle (the pie) with different sized **sectors** (the slices of the pie).

Here is a pie chart showing how Jenny spends her day.

How Jenny Spends her Day

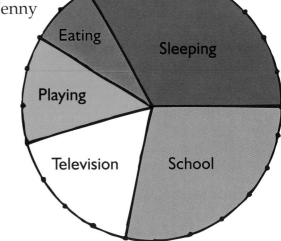

Activity	Hours
Sleeping	8
Eating	2
Playing	3
Watching TV	4
At School	7

Of the 24 hours in the day, Jenny spends 3 hours playing. This is one-eighth of her day. So the slice of the pie that represents her "playing" is one-eighth of the whole pie. She spends 8 hours sleeping, which is one-third of her day. So the slice of the pie that represents her "sleeping" is one-third of the whole pie.

The size of each sector (slice) is a fraction of the whole circle that matches the fraction of time spent on each activity in Jenny's day.

TO DO

- Draw your own pie chart to show how you spent yesterday.
- Start by writing the data in a table.
- Draw a circle with a circular **protractor**, and divide the boundary of the circle into 24 equal divisions, one for each hour of the day. To do this, you need to make a mark for every 15°, since 360° ÷ 24 is 15°.
- Then use the data in your table to draw the different sized sectors. Label each sector.

Data can be collected by asking people questions and recording their answers.

Gary is collecting data to find out twelve classmates' favorite sports. This pie chart shows the results.

Gary's Classmates' Favorite Sports

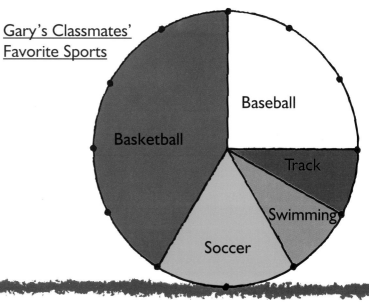

CHALLENGE

What does the pie chart tell you about how Gary's classmates voted?

TO DO

- Draw two circles and divide the boundary of each into 18 equal parts (by drawing around a circular **protractor** and marking every 20°).
- Take a deck of cards, shuffle them, and deal out eighteen.
- On the first circle, draw a pie chart to show how many cards you have of each suit: hearts, clubs, diamonds, and spades.
- On the second circle, draw a pie chart to show how many picture cards, odd-numbered, and even-numbered cards you have.
- Label each chart.

9 CONVERSION GRAPHS

A **conversion graph** is a line graph used to convert from one unit of measurement to another unit of measurement.

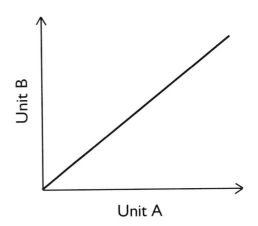

Long distances are sometimes measured in miles, and sometimes measured in kilometers.

80 kilometers is the same distance as 50 miles.

In the United States, long distance is measured in miles, but in many other countries, kilometers are used. If you need to convert distances from miles to kilometers, or kilometers to miles, a conversion graph will help you do both.

Conversion Graph for Miles and Kilometers

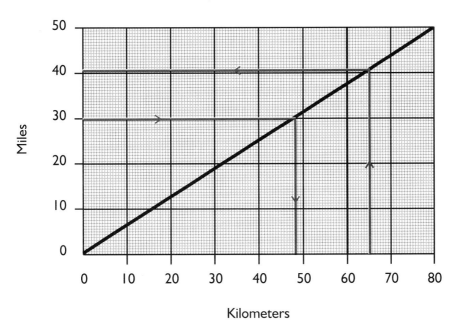

The graph shows you two conversions:
- the number of kilometers in 30 miles – 48 kilometers
- the number of miles in 65 kilometers – about 40 miles.

TO DO

- Use the graph above to find how many kilometers there are in 20 miles and 35 miles.
- Use the graph to find how many miles there are in 20 kilometers and 55 kilometers.

CHALLENGE

Here is a different conversion graph. It converts one currency, British pounds (£), to another, U.S. dollars ($).

- Convert £5 into dollars.
- Convert $10 into pounds.

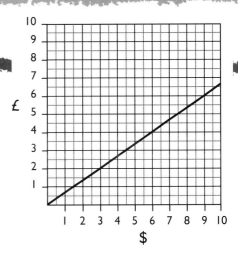

21

VENN DIAGRAMS

A **Venn diagram** is a chart used to sort data. All Venn diagrams start with a rectangle, inside which are a number of circles that sometimes cross each other (intersect). Some examples of Venn diagrams are shown in the diagram below.

 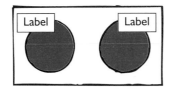 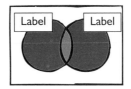 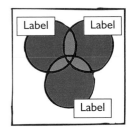

Each circle represents a set of objects or numbers, depending on what kind of data is being sorted. Each circle should be clearly labeled.

Instead of drawing the Venn diagram, the rectangle can be represented by a table top and the circles by hoops. Objects can then be sorted onto the table.

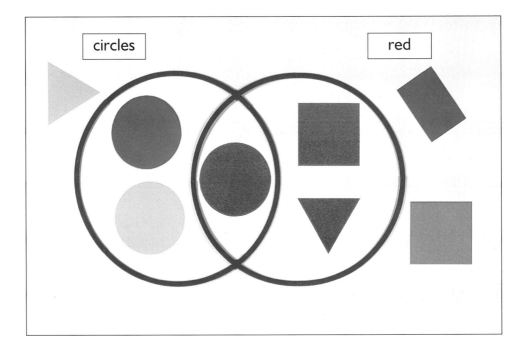

Where should a red rectangle go?
Where should a blue triangle go?

When the shapes have been sorted into the Venn diagram, each region contains a particular collection of shapes that can be clearly described.

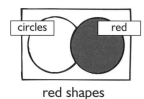

red shapes

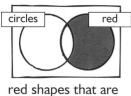

red shapes that are
not circles

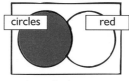

circles

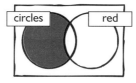

circles that are
not red

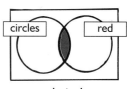

red circles

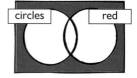

shapes that are neither
circles nor red

CHALLENGE

This Venn diagram has three circles, one for each of these sets of numbers: odd numbers, numbers more than 6, and numbers less than 12.

Two numbers are in the wrong place. What are they, and where should they go?

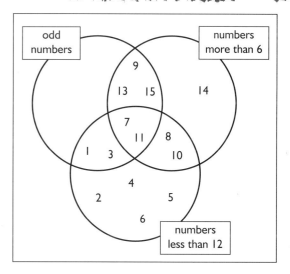

TO DO

You need a deck of cards.
- Draw three large intersecting circles inside a rectangle, like the Venn diagram above.
- Label the circles "red," "hearts," and "picture cards."
- Sort the cards into their correct positions on the Venn diagram.
- Try inventing your own labels for the three circles, then sorting the cards.

DATABASES

A **database** is a collection of lots of different data about the same subjects.

Claire	Siobhan	Bejal	Jack
8 years old	10 years old	11 years old	10 years old
1 brother	0 brothers	1 brother	1 brother
2 sisters	1 sister	0 sisters	3 sisters
blue eyes	blue eyes	brown eyes	brown eyes
red hair	blond hair	black hair	brown hair

All of this information can be put into a table. This table is called a database.

Name	Claire	Siobhan	Bejal	Jack
Age	8	10	11	10
Brothers	1	0	1	1
Sisters	2	1	0	3
Eye Color	blue	blue	brown	brown
Hair Color	red	blond	black	brown

The database makes it easier to search for and find information.

TO DO

Use the table to answer the following questions.
- How many of the children have blue eyes?
- How many are 9 or more years old?
- How many have no brothers?
- How many have more sisters than brothers?
- Who has brown eyes and brown hair?

- Create a list of your own personal facts. Here are some examples of data that you might record.

Name	Height	House number	Favorite drink
Brothers	Weight	Phone number	Favorite color
Sisters	Hair color	Lucky number	Favorite TV show
Age	Eye color	Favorite food	Favorite music

- Collect data from your friends and build a table for your own database.

A soccer league table is another example of a database. The data in the table summarizes current standing of each team in the league.

Team	Matches Won	Matches Tied	Matches Lost	Goals Scored	Goals Conceded	Points
Stars	22	12	7	74	42	78
Champs	23	8	9	73	32	77
Lightning	20	12	6	70	30	72
Cougars	18	15	7	62	35	69
Ramblers	19	11	11	61	48	68
Striders	20	6	13	69	63	66

The teams are awarded 3 points for a win, 1 point for a tie, and 0 points for a loss.

CHALLENGE

Look at the league table above.
- Which team scored the fewest goals? Which the most?
- Which team tied the most matches? Which tied the least often?
- Which team has the largest difference between goals scored and goals conceded (given up)?
- Suppose there were only 2 points for a win instead of 3. How many points would each team have? Would they be in the same positions in the league?

TO DO

Create a database to show the results of these matches in the form of a league table:

Lincoln 2 Harrison 1

Harrison 2 Sunnydale 3

Clarkton 1 Madison 0

Madison 0 Lincoln 0

Sunnydale 3 Madison 3

Lincoln 1 Clarkton 1

Harrison 4 Madison 5

Sunnydale 3 Lincoln 1

Clarkton 1 Harrison 4

Sunnydale 2 Clarkton 2

DECISION TREES

A **decision tree** can be used to sort objects. It is called a tree because it has several branches (or routes). At the start of a pair of branches is a question to which the answer is either "Yes" or "No." This is where you have to make the decisions.

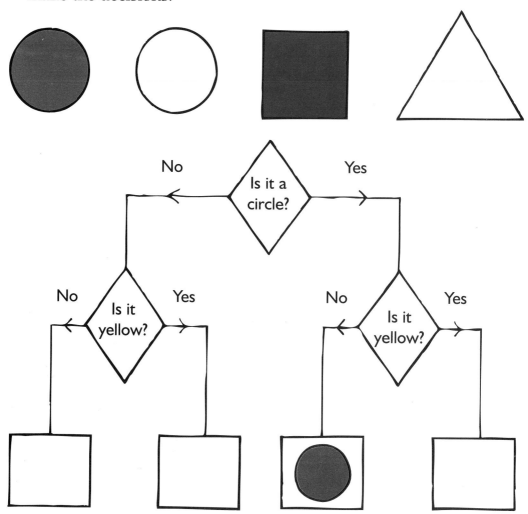

This decision tree will sort the shapes.
Start by sorting the red circle.
The answer to the first question, "Is it a circle?" is "Yes."
Follow the branch until you come to the next question,
"Is it yellow?" The answer is "No."

TO DO

Sort the other shapes to decide where they go.

A deck of cards can be sorted in many different ways.

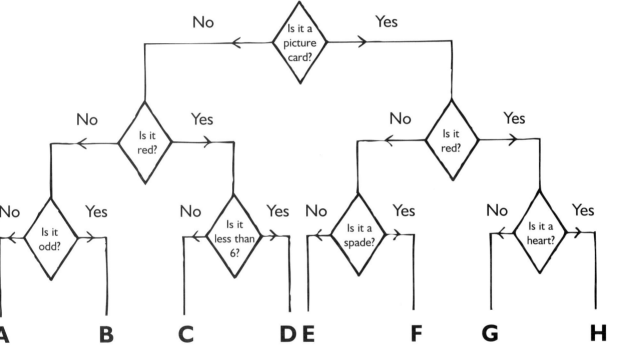

CHALLENGE

Take a deck of cards, shuffle them, then try each in turn using the decision tree. Find out how many cards will finish in each of the eight positions labeled A to H.

TO DO

Invent your own decision tree to sort a deck of cards, then try it out.

AVERAGES

An **average** of a set of numbers is a middle number about which they are centered. For example, the average of the numbers 27, 29, 35, 38, 24, 30, and 34 is 31.

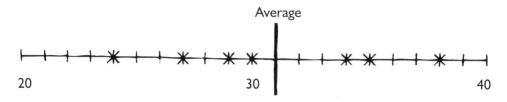

To find the average of a set of numbers, find their total and divide this by the number in the set. The set of numbers 3, 4, and 8, for example, has a total of 15, and there are three of them. So their average is 15 ÷ 3, which is 5.

The average of a set of numbers is often not a whole number. The set of numbers 7, 2, 6, and 3, for example, has a total of 18, and there are four of them. So their average is 18 ÷ 4, which is 4.5.

This average is sometimes called the **mean**.

TO DO

Play the Average Number Cube Game.

You need five number cubes.

• Take turns throwing the cubes. You may choose to throw 2, 3, 4, or 5 cubes at the same time.

• Your score is the average cube number to the nearest whole number. For example, if you choose 3 cubes and throw this

 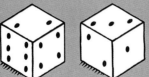 pattern, then the total is 11. There are 3 cubes, so the average is 11 ÷ 3, which is 4 to the nearest whole number. This is your score.

• The player with the highest average wins the round.

• Check each other's scores.

• The winner is the first to win six rounds.

The average contents of a box of paperclips is stated on the box.

"Average Contents: 40" means that some boxes may have a few less than 40 paperclips, and some a few more, but overall, the number of paperclips in a box will be close to 40.

TO DO

Find the average number of letters in a word.

Alice was beginning to get very tired of sitting by her sister on the bank, and of having nothing to do: once or twice she had peeped into the book her sister was reading, but it had no pictures or conversations in it, "and what is the use of a book," thought Alice, "without pictures or conversation?" So she was considering in her own mind (as well as she could, for the hot day made her feel very sleepy and stupid), whether the pleasure of making a daisy chain would be worth the trouble of getting up and picking the ...

Here are a hundred words from a book.
The number of letters in the first few words are:
5, 3, 9, 2, 3. Use a tally chart to record the number of letters in all the hundred words, and use this to find the average number of letters in a word.

CHALLENGE

Find the average number of letters in another book or newspaper. Compare this average with the average found above.

SCHEDULES

Useful data is presented in the form of a schedule. If you are planning to go to the movies, then you need to know what films are showing and at what time they start.

CHALLENGE

Study the movie schedule. The movie "Little Men" is shown three times on a Friday and four times on every other day. The movie lasts for 2 hours and 15 minutes.

- How much time is there between when the movie ends and when it starts again?
- How many times is it shown in a week?
- How many times are the other movies shown in the week?
- How many movie showings are there on each day of the week? How many in the week altogether?
- Which is the longest movie?
- Which is the shortest?

Quiet and Quieter (12) 2 hrs
(two screens)

| Fri/Sat | 1:00 1:45 3:30 4:15 6:00 7:00 8:30 9:40 10:55 12:00 |
| Sun–Thurs | 11:15 1:00 1:45 3:30 4:15 6:00 7:00 8:30 9:40 |

Little Men (66) 2 hrs 15 mins

| Fri | 2:00 5:00 8:00 |
| Sat–Thurs | 11:30 2:00 5:00 8:00 |

Enclosure (18) 2 hrs 20 mins

| Fri/Sat | 12:00 3:20 6:20 9:15 11:50 |
| Sun–Thurs | 12:00 3:20 6:20 9:15 |

Small Adventure (15) 2 hrs 5 mins

| Fri/Sat | 2:10 4:40 7:20 9:50 |
| Sun–Thurs | 11:45 2:10 4:40 7:20 9:50 |

Terminal Speed (15) 2 hrs

| Fri/Sat | 7:30 10:00 12:10 |
| Sun–Thurs | 1:45 12:45 3:00 |

1001 Puppies (66) 1 hr 35 mins

| Daily | 10:15 12:30 2:45 5:10 |

Near to Work (66) 1 hr 35 mins

| Fri/Sat | 12:45 3:00 |
| Sun–Thurs | 10:45 12:45 3:00 |

Kindness of Jim (PG) 2 hrs 10 mins

| Daily | 12:10 2:30 5:30 8:15 |

TO DO

Find a movie schedule from the local newspaper and analyze the data.

In the same way, if you are going to watch television you need to find out what programs will be on, the times they start, and the times they finish.

CHALLENGE

Look at the television schedule below:
- Which program starts at 8:55?
- Which program finishes at 7:10?
- Which program comes after "Private Lives"?
- How long does "Cat and Mouse" last?
- How many programs could you watch between 5:00 and 8:00 in the evening?
- Which programs last for exactly half an hour?
- How many last for longer than half an hour?
- How many last for less than half an hour?
- Which program is the longest?
- How long does each program last?

Saturday

7:25 News; Weather	5:15 News; Weather
7:30 Pingo (rept)	5:25 Local News
7:35 Cat and Mouse	5:30 Cartoon
7:50 The Five Musketeers	5:50 Quiz Show
8:15 Joketime	6:20 Music Time
8:35 The Baboons	7:10 Private Lives
9:00 Playtime	7:50 Lottery
12:12 Saturday Sports	8:05 Nasties
12:20 *Racing*	8:55 News; Sports; Weather
12:30 *Soccer*	9:15 Cops
12:40 *Tennis*	10:00 Bob Smith Show
1:00 *News*	10:40 Match of the Day
1:05 *Baseball*	11:40 Comedians
3:05 *Football*	12:10 Movie
4:00 *Golf*	1:50 News; Weather
4:40 *Results*	

DISTANCE CHARTS

A **distance chart** allows you to find the distance between two towns or cities.

If you were going on a trip to Great Britain, then you need to know how far it is from one town to another, and how long it will take you to get there.

CHALLENGE

Do you think it is farther from Oxford to Leeds than it is from Gloucester to Harwich?
A distance chart will help you find out.

Distance Chart in Miles

	London	Birmingham	Bournemouth	Brighton	Bristol	Cardiff	Croyden	Dover	Edinburgh	Exeter	Glasgow	Gloucester	Harwich	Leeds	Liverpool	Newcastle	Norwich	Nottingham	Oxford	Plymouth	Portsmouth	Sheffield	Southampton	Stockport	Stoke on Trent
Birmingham	120																								
Bournemouth	104	145																							
Brighton	57	183	94																						
Bristol	118	89	75	167																					
Cardiff	153	110	126	203	47																				
Croyden	14	157	117	43	142	178																			
Dover	79	202	180	83	205	240	78																		
Edinburgh	405	291	438	468	373	394	442	487																	
Exeter	198	162	84	171	82	120	191	254	446																
Glasgow	402	288	435	464	370	390	439	484	46	443															
Gloucester	105	54	104	162	35	57	137	199	338	108	335														
Harwich	82	168	201	132	215	251	90	130	418	295	425	190													
Leeds	197	133	256	260	215	236	234	279	210	288	247	180	220												
Liverpool	213	98	246	275	180	202	250	295	222	253	219	145	261	73											
Newcastle	286	204	345	347	298	319	322	350	112	371	149	263	302	94	184										
Norwich	115	163	230	177	244	280	134	175	374	324	380	184	74	175	219	257									
Nottingham	129	57	188	191	151	172	166	211	277	224	283	116	162	72	110	160	122								
Oxford	57	65	93	108	73	108	83	145	358	150	354	48	142	164	165	252	144	96							
Plymouth	238	202	126	213	123	160	232	294	486	44	483	148	330	328	294	411	336	264	193						
Portsmouth	72	148	51	50	96	142	78	140	451	128	448	117	174	247	258	335	204	179	83	171					
Sheffield	169	89	228	232	182	203	206	251	250	255	257	147	196	35	79	134	152	44	136	295	219				
Southampton	77	130	32	63	76	122	90	152	433	109	429	99	174	229	240	317	202	161	65	150	19	201			
Stockport	199	85	233	262	167	188	237	281	224	241	221	132	223	58	41	169	178	66	152	280	245	38	227		
Stoke on Trent	159	45	194	222	128	150	196	241	249	201	246	93	208	91	56	202	172	51	112	241	206	52	188	43	
Watford	21	102	110	82	125	160	57	114	387	205	384	99	93	179	195	267	123	111	51	244	84	151	82	181	141

To find the distance between two towns, look at the square in which the row and column meet. For example, to find the distance between Cardiff and Norwich, look down the Cardiff column, until you meet the Norwich row. The meeting square shows you that the two towns are 280 miles apart.

TO DO

- Find five pairs of towns that are more than 300 miles apart.
- Find five pairs of towns that are less than 50 miles apart.

16 TIMETABLES

A **timetable** provides data to help you plan a trip.
This is a timetable for the number 51 bus.

BANKS BROOK - CITY MOOR - CROSSTOWN - HILLTOWN - GOLDHILL 51					
Elm St. Station	6:25	6:55	7:25	7:55	9:15
Pine St.	6:30	7:00	7:30	8:00	9:20
Oak St.	6:41	7:11	7:41	8:11	9:31
Chestnut St.	6:50	7:20	7:50	8:20	9:40
Madison Ave.	6:55	7:25	7:55	8:25	9:45
Adams Ave.	7:05	7:35	8:05	8:35	9:55
Douglass Ave.	7:12	7:42	8:12	8:42	10:02
Houston Ave.	7:20	7:50	8:20	8:50	10:10
Lincoln Ave.	7:25	7:55	8:25	8:55	10:15
King Station	7:30	8:00	8:30	9:00	10:20

To read the times of a bus trip, you need to look at a
column of times.
The first column looks like this:

Elm St. Station	6:25
Pine St.	6:30
Oak St.	6:41
Chestnut St.	6:50
Madison Ave.	6:55
Adams Ave.	7:05
Douglass Ave.	7:12
Houston Ave.	7:20
Lincoln Ave.	7:25
King Station	7:30

This is the first bus in the morning. It leaves Elm Street
Station at 6:25 in the morning, and arrives at King Station
at 7:30. *How long does the whole trip take?*

CHALLENGE

Can you figure out how long the bus takes to travel from:
• Pine St. to Chestnut St.
• Chestnut St. to Douglass Ave.
• Madison Ave. to Lincoln Ave.?
Some timetables, for example, airlines schedules, follow a 24-hour clock. In a 24-hour clock, the morning hours are the same as a 12-hour clock—9:00, 10:00, 11:00, up until 12:00, noon. But 1:00 in the afternoon is written as 13:00, 2:00 in the afternoon is written as 14:00, and so on.
How would you write 5:00 in the afternoon using a 24-hour clock?

CHICAGO FLIGHT ARRIVALS				
Flight No.	From	Departs	Arrives	Status
2345	Omaha	9:15	11:20	on time
2789	Indianapolis	10:25	11:10	on time
409	Minn/St. Paul	11:45	13:00	on time
1003	Dallas	12:15	14:15	on time
2315	New Orleans	12:05	14:00	on time
1755	Kansas City	12:30	14:15	on time

This airline schedule shows what time a flight leaves a city and when it will arrive in Chicago. It follows a 24-hour clock. For example, Flight No. 2789 from Indianapolis leaves at 10:25 in the morning and arrives at 11:10 in the morning. Flight 409 from Minneapolis/St. Paul leaves at 11:45 in the morning and arrives at 13:00, or 1:00 in the afternoon.

CHALLENGE

How long does it take to fly from Dallas to Chicago?
How long from New Orleans? How long from Kansas City?

CHANCE AND PROBABILITY

If something may or may not happen, you sometimes need to decide how likely it is to happen. This is called the **chance** or **probability** that it will happen.

- *Will it rain tomorrow?*
- *Will you grow up to be taller than your mother?*
- *Will you become famous?*

If it has a good chance of happening, it is more likely to happen than not. If it has a poor chance of happening, it is less likely to happen than not.

If it has an **even chance** of happening, it is as likely to happen as not. This even chance is sometimes called a fifty-fifty chance.

If it has no chance of happening, it is impossible. If it is sure to happen, it is certain.

TO DO

What are the chances of these things happening to you?

Use the words "impossible," "poor chance," "even chance," "good chance," and "certain."

I will visit Australia	I will travel in a rocket	It will rain this year	I will turn into a frog
It will get dark tonight	I will get younger everyday	I will one day be married	I will learn to drive a car
I will live for 100 years	I will become a teacher	I will appear on television	I will grow to be 6 feet tall

These different chances can be shown in order on a line.

If this line is matched to a number line from 0 to 1, then the positions of the chances on the line are called **probabilities**.

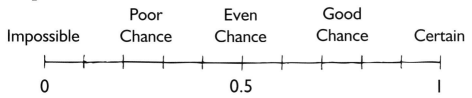

- If something is impossible, its probability is 0.
- If something is certain, its probability is 1.
- If something has a fifty-fifty chance of happening, its probability is $\frac{1}{2}$.
- If something has a good chance of happening, its probability is between $\frac{1}{2}$ and 1.

A probability is a number between 0 and 1. The probability that something will happen is a measure of its chance of happening.

TO DO

Play the Probability Game.

- Start by making twelve probability cards, three of each of these:

| Probability is 0 | Probability is between 0 and $\frac{1}{2}$ | Probability is between $\frac{1}{2}$ and 1 | Probability is 1 |

- Shuffle the cards and place them in a pile face down.
- Take turns to reveal the top card, such as,

| Probability is between $\frac{1}{2}$ and 1 |

Throw a number cube, such as,

- Use the key on the right to match the cube number to a time: "tomorrow afternoon."

- Invent an outcome for your partner to match the probability card and the time, such as, "Tomorrow afternoon you will smile."
- Discuss each other's statements to see if you agree.

Key

Next Saturday

This evening

Tomorrow afternoon

In the year 2000

Next week

Next Christmas

PROBABILITY: NUMBER CUBES

A six-faced number cube is used in many games of chance because when it is rolled, each face has an equal chance of appearing.

This tally chart shows the results of rolling a cube 60 times.

Number	Tallies	Frequency
1	‖‖ ‖‖	9
2	‖‖ ‖‖	8
3	‖‖ ‖‖ ‖‖	12
4	‖‖ ‖‖	10
5	‖‖ ‖‖ ‖‖	13
6	‖‖ ‖‖	8

Since each face of the number cube has an equal chance of appearing, it is expected that approximately one sixth of all the throws will show 1, another sixth will show 2, and so on. As the cube was rolled 60 times, we expect approximately ten of each number. We expect them to be near to ten, but very rarely will they be exactly ten.

We say: "The probability of throwing a 1 is $\frac{1}{6}$."
So is the probability of throwing a 2, 3, 4, 5, or a 6.

TO DO

- Roll a number cube 120 times, but first decide how many times you expect each number to appear.
- Record your results in a table and compare the totals with your expectations.

TO DO

Play the Horse Race Game.

You need counters and a red and a green number cube.

- Start by drawing a large version of the race track below.
- Place a counter (the horse) at the start of each track.
- Throw both cubes, find the total, and move the matching horse forward one space.
- Continue throwing the cubes and moving a matching horse one space.
- The winning horse is the first to reach "Finish."

Play several games and see which are the winning horses. Do some horses have better chances of winning than others?

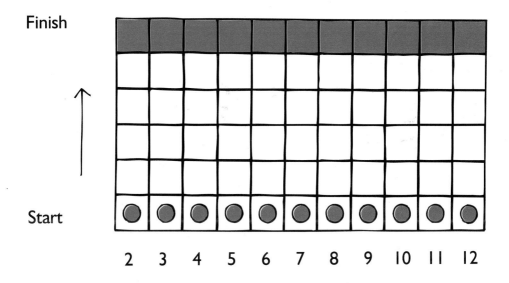

PROBABILITY: TOSSING COINS

When a coin is tossed, it can land either heads or tails. Each is equally likely. Each has an even chance. Each has a probability of $\frac{1}{2}$.

When two coins are tossed, sometimes both will show heads, sometimes both will show tails, and sometimes there will be one head and one tail.

TO DO

You need a nickel and a penny.
• Toss the nickel first, then the penny.
• Do this twenty times and see how may of the tosses result in both heads (HH), how many in both tails (TT) and how many in one of each (HT or TH).

The different possible happenings are as follows:

Nickel	Penny	
Head	Head	(HH)
Head	Tail	(HT)
Tail	Head	(TH)
Tail	Tail	(TT)

All of these are equally likely.
So approximately one quarter of the tosses should show two heads, another quarter should show two tails, and a half of the tosses should show a head and a tail. Compare this with the results of your twenty throws.

The probability of tossing two heads is $\frac{1}{4}$.
The probability of tossing two tails is $\frac{1}{4}$.
The probability of tossing a head and a tail is $\frac{1}{2}$.

40

When three coins are tossed, the different possible happenings or outcomes can be shown by a **tree diagram**. First a dime is tossed, then a nickel, and finally a quarter.

Tree Diagram for Tossing 3 Coins

Dime	Nickel	Quarter	Outcome
	H	H	HHH
		T	HHT
H	T	H	HTH
		T	HTT
	H	H	THH
		T	THT
T	T	H	TTH
		T	TTT

There are eight different paths from left to right along the "branches of the tree."

Each path shows one of the eight different possible outcomes. Each outcome is equally likely, and so each has a probability of $\frac{1}{8}$.

One of the eight outcomes results in no heads at all: TTT.

Three of these outcomes result in one head: HTT, THT, TTH.

Three result in two heads: HTH, HHT, THH.

One results in three heads: HHH.

These can lead to a probability table.

Probability Table for Tossing 3 Coins

Number of Heads	Probability
0	$\frac{1}{8}$
1	$\frac{3}{8}$
2	$\frac{3}{8}$
3	$\frac{1}{8}$

TO DO

You need a dime, a nickel and a quarter.
- Toss the three coins 24 times altogether.
- Count the number of times you throw 0 heads, 1 head, 2 heads, and 3 heads.
- Compare your results with your expectations.

CHOICES

Sometimes when we have a choice, we need to know how many different possible choices can be made.

Sandwiches

Fillings: Ham
           Cheese and tomato
           Chicken

Bread: White
        Rye

One possible choice is a ham sandwich on white bread. Another is a chicken sandwich on rye bread.

There are six different possible choices altogether. *What are the other four?*

Menu

Fish sticks or sausages

- - - - - - - - - - - -

Fries, boiled potatoes, or mashed potatoes

- - - - - - - - - - - -

Beans or peas

Karen chose sausages, mashed potatoes, and beans.
John chose fish sticks, fries, and peas.
What would you choose?

Can you find twelve different choices altogether?

When choosing a sandwich, there were 3 fillings and 2 types of bread, giving 3 x 2 = 6 different choices.
When choosing from the menu, there were 2 main dishes, 3 types of potato, and 2 vegetables, giving 2 x 3 x 2 = 12 different choices.

If you are organizing a tournament, you need to know how many matches need to be scheduled.

There is going to be a checkers competition for five players. Each player must play every other player, and we need to know how many matches will be played altogether.

If the five players are labelled A, B, C, D, and E, we can work systematically by:
- listing all of A's matches
- then listing B's remaining matches, not counting the match against A
- then listing C's remaining matches, and then D's.

All of E's matches should now be listed.

    A v B   B v C   C v D   D v E
    A v C   B v D   C v E
    A v D   B v E
    A v E

There are 10 matches altogether. Check that none are missing.

Each match can be shown by a line joining two points on this diagram. Check that there are 10.

The matches can also be shown on a chart like this. The shaded squares show the 10 matches.

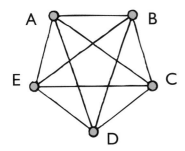

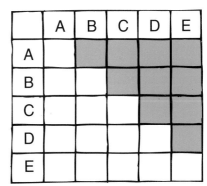

CHALLENGE:

- Four people are in a room and each must shake the hand of the other three people. Find how many handshakes there will be altogether.
- Extend the problem to five people and then to six.
- Can you spot a pattern in the number of handshakes each time?

GLOSSARY

average	A number about which numbered data is centered.
axes	The two lines that explain the data being shown on a graph. One line is **horizontal** and one is **vertical**.
bar graph	A graph that uses bars to show the data. The heights of the bars show frequencies.
bar graph with lines	A graph in which the bars have been replaced by lines.
block graph	A graph that uses blocks to show the data.
chance	The chance of something happening is how likely it is to happen.
conversion graph	A line graph used to convert from one unit of measurement to another.
database	A large collection of data that can be sorted in different ways.
data	Facts and information about something.
data collection sheet	A sheet for recording data.
data processing	Simplifying and ordering recorded data.
data representation	Showing the data in an easy-to-read way.
decision tree	A chart that has different routes (branches) to follow after answering questions.
distance chart	A chart that helps you find the distance between two places.
distance-time graph	A line graph in which the axes are distance and time.
even chance	Equally likely to happen as not to happen.
frequency	How many or how often.
grouped data	Sets of scores or observations put together into groups.
horizontal line	A straight line drawn from left to right on the paper.
interpreting data	Reading and understanding data.
key	A guide to explain the meaning of part of a graph.

line graph	A graph with a continuous line or lines to show trends or changes.
mean	An average.
pictograph	A graph that uses pictures to show data.
pie chart	A graph or chart that shows data by slicing a pie (circle) into slices (sectors).
probability	A measure of chance, between 0 and 1.
protractor	An instrument for measuring angles.
questionnaire	A set of questions used to collect data.
sector	A slice of a pie chart.
tally	Line or marks to score the number of times something occurs.
tally chart	A chart or table for drawing tallies.
timetable	A chart showing times for different parts of a journey or event.
tree diagram	A chart with "branches of a tree" to show different possible happenings.
Venn diagram	A chart that sorts data by placing it in circles.
vertical line	A straight line drawn from the top to bottom, at right angles to a horizontal line.

INDEX

ANSWERS

p. 6   Mint, 5 shoppers; Vanilla was the most popular flavor.

p. 7   Summer 10; autumn 6; winter 3; altogether 26

p. 8   **To Do**
11; 4; 13

p. 9   **Challenge**
30-39; 4; 31; 18

p. 11   **To Do**
2, brown and black; 3; 11

p. 13   **Challenge**
One possible solution is:

p. 16   **To Do**
70°F, 75°F; 12:00 and 3:00; 1°F increase;
between 1:00 and 2:00.

p. 19   **Challenge**
Baseball – 3 votes, Track – 1 vote, Swimming – 1 vote,
Soccer – 2 votes, Basketball – 5 votes.

p. 21   32km and 54km; 12.5 miles and 34.5 miles.

Challenge
$7.50; £6,50

p. 23   5 and 9 are in the wrong place.

p. 24   2; 3; 1; 3; Jack.

p. 25   **Challenge**
Ramblers; Stars; Cougers; Striders; Champs;
Stars, 56; Champs, 54; Lightning, 52;
Cougers, 51; Ramblers, 49; Striders, 46.

p. 29   Average of 4 letters in a word.

p. 30	45 mins; 27; Quiet and Quieter, 65; Little Men, 27; Enclosure, 30; Small Adventure, 33; Terminal Speed, 21; 1001 Puppies, 28; Near to Work, 19; Kindness of Jim, 28. 36 every day except 35 on Friday. Longest - "Enclosure," shortest - "1001 Puppies" and "Near to Work."
p. 32	Gloucester to Harwich is farther.
p. 34	65 minutes (1 hour and 5 minutes).
p. 35	**Challenge** 20 minutes; 22 minutes; 30 minutes 17:00 **Challenge** 2 hours; 1 hour, 55 minutes; 1 hour, 45 minutes.
p. 42	Ham on rye; cheese and tomato on rye; chicken on white; cheese and tomato on white. Fish sticks, fries, beans. Fish sticks, boiled potatoes, beans. Fish sticks, mashed potatoes, beans. Fish sticks, fries, peas. Fish sticks, boiled potatoes, peas. Fish sticks, mashed potatoes, peas. Sausages, fries, beans. Sausages, boiled potatoes, beans. Sausages, mashed potatoes, beans. Sausages, fries, peas. Sausages, boiled potatoes, peas. Sausages, mashed potatoes, peas.
p. 43	**Challenge** handshakes: 4 people, 6; 5 people, 10; 6 people, 15.